Zebras are among the most beautiful animals on earth. With their bold black-and-white stripes, they stand apart from every other kind of animal. In Africa, where all zebras live, thundering herds of these magnificent animals roam freely over the vast plains.

Many people don't know it, but the zebra is one of the few wild horses left in the world today. All horses, both domestic and wild, belong to the animal group, or genus, known as *Equus*.

Like all horses, zebras have long, handsome faces with big, gentle eyes. They have strong bodies and long, slender legs. And once they get going, they can run with a speed and grace that is truly wonderful to watch.

Zebras are shorter than most other horses, and they have smaller hooves. Their manes are stiff, their ears are large, and some of them bark! (Zebras that live on the plains make a kwa-ha-ha noise, so one of them was named the quagga, in imitation of the sound it made.) Most important, *only* zebras have stripes—*even their manes are striped*!

As you will see, there are three different types of zebras—and each type lives in a different part of Africa. *Plains zebras* are found on the open grasslands and along the edges of deserts from eastern Africa across to southwestern Africa. *Mountain zebras* live in the stony mountains of southern Africa. And *Grevy's zebras* live in the dry semi-deserts of northeast Africa.

Plains zebras are the most common zebras. There are fewer Grevy's zebras—also considered the most primitive of the zebra species—and *even fewer* mountain zebras. Two zebras that once crowded the African plains are extinct. Why have some zebras disappeared?

The biggest reason is that people have turned the wild lands into farms and ranches. This limits the amount of open space where zebras can run free. Many zebras have been killed for their beautiful skins.

Fortunately, things are being done to protect zebras now. African governments and wildlife organizations have set up nature preserves, where zebras can live without the risk of being hunted. This is an important step toward saving these beautiful animals in the wild.

Most zebras live on the open grasslands, where there is plenty to eat, but few places to hide from predators. To stay alive, zebras must be able to *make quick getaways* when a predator creeps up.

The legs of zebras are very long, so when they run they can take big strides. And they have strong muscles and large lungs, so they can keep running for long distances without tiring or slowing down.

Zebras are plant-eating animals, or *herbivores*. As you will see below, they have extra long necks to help them reach the grass on the ground. And they have special teeth to help them chew their food.

A zebra has several speeds, or *gaits*. Each gait requires the animal to move its legs in a different pattern. The most important gaits for running are the *trot* and the *gallop*.

When grazing, zebras use their sharp front teeth like scissors to clip off the grass. Usually, they eat only the tips of the grass.

The bones of a zebra are lightweight, but strong. As thin as a zebra's leg may look, it is actually strong enough to support all of the animal's weight when it gallops. And zebras are heavy—some weigh as much as 950 pounds.

The strong back teeth, or *molars*, are used to crush and grind coarse grass. When chewing, the lower jaw moves against the upper jaw in a sideways motion. A zebra's back teeth keep growing until the animal reaches old age, so they almost never wear out.

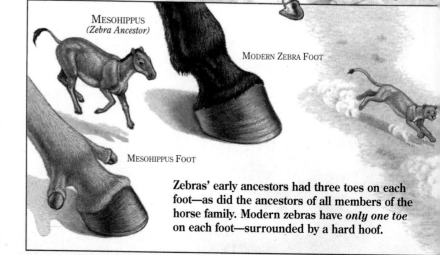

MESOHIPPUS
(Zebra Ancestor)

MODERN ZEBRA FOOT

MESOHIPPUS FOOT

Zebras' early ancestors had three toes on each foot—as did the ancestors of all members of the horse family. Modern zebras have *only one toe* on each foot—surrounded by a hard hoof.

e trot is a fairly fast but easy gait that zebras
e for traveling long distances—for example,
en looking for new pastures. In the trot, the
agonal legs move together—first one pair,
en the other.

A zebra's fastest gait is the gallop. In the gallop, all four hooves may be off the ground at once for a split second. Then, one after the other, each foot touches down with a sharp, quick thud. When running from predators, zebras can gallop 35 miles an hour or more.

To reach the grass on the ground, zebras have long heads and necks. Yet a zebra has only seven bones in its neck—the same number that you have in yours!

Because zebras have narrow feet and hard hooves, they can run over rocky ground that would hurt the feet of most other kinds of animals.

The running muscles of a zebra are bunched near the shoulders and hips, rather than down the legs, where their weight would slow the animal down. Tough, cord-like tendons attach the zebra's running muscles to its leg bones. When the muscles contract, the legs move.

A zebra's life is full of danger from hungry lions, leopards, hyenas, and wild dogs. Most of the time, these predators hunt by sneaking up on their prey and then catching it by surprise. To be safe from them, zebras must *stay alert at all times*.

Luckily, zebras have wonderful senses to help them detect enemies before they attack. Their excellent eyesight, hearing, and sense of smell all help to warn them when predators are nearby.

A zebra can easily outrun a predator over a long distance. As it runs, the zebra zigzags from side to side, looking back over its shoulder to see if the predator is still behind it. If the zebra can get away in the first 100 yards, it is usually home free.

When a zebra is attacked, it fights for its life—kicking har with its hind legs and biting with its teeth. A zebra can kil a leopard with one well-place kick. But often it is the leopa that wins the fight.

Zebras have excellent hearing to listen for predators. They can twist their flexible ears in almost any direction to pick up sounds all around them.

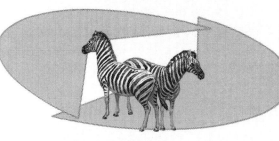

The eyes of a zebra are set high on the sides of its head to allow a wide range of vision. Even when bending down to graze, zebras can look out over the grass to watch for predators.

When two zebras stand side by side, they usually face in opposite directions. This makes it possible for them to see in *all directions*—and makes it twice as easy to spot predators.

All zebras seem to know when a lion is hungry and when it is just resting. So they will often graze very peacefully when lions are around—but always at a safe distance.

Danger lurks everywhere for zebras—even in the water. A hungry crocodile in a water hole will grab a zebra in a second if it has a chance.

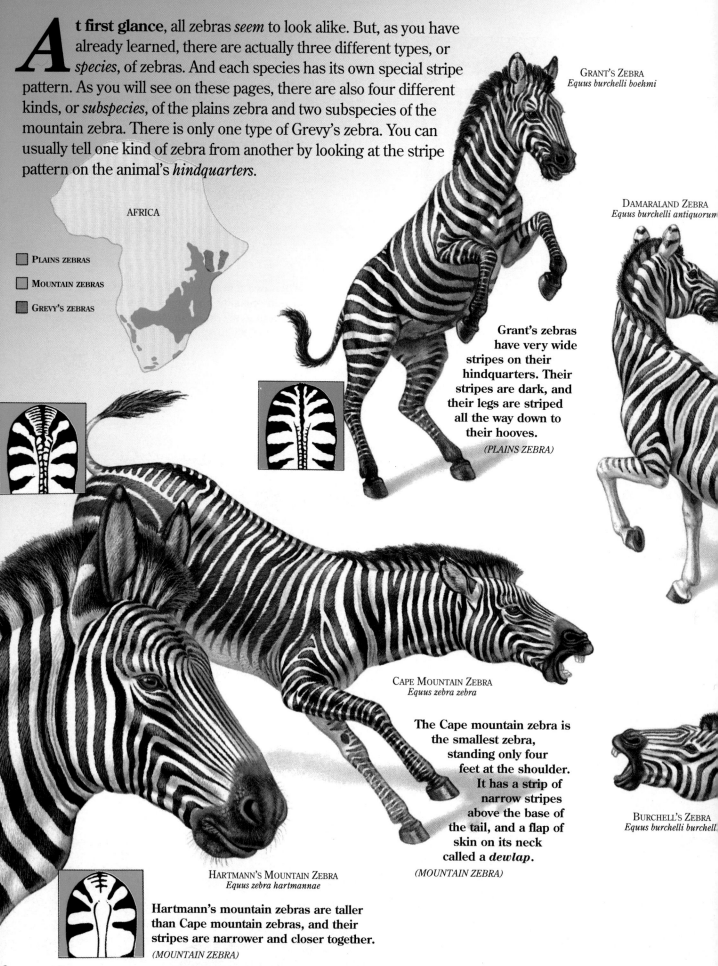

At first glance, all zebras *seem* to look alike. But, as you have already learned, there are actually three different types, or *species*, of zebras. And each species has its own special stripe pattern. As you will see on these pages, there are also four different kinds, or *subspecies*, of the plains zebra and two subspecies of the mountain zebra. There is only one type of Grevy's zebra. You can usually tell one kind of zebra from another by looking at the stripe pattern on the animal's *hindquarters*.

AFRICA

☐ PLAINS ZEBRAS
☐ MOUNTAIN ZEBRAS
☐ GREVY'S ZEBRAS

GRANT'S ZEBRA
Equus burchelli boehmi

DAMARALAND ZEBRA
Equus burchelli antiquorum

Grant's zebras have very wide stripes on their hindquarters. Their stripes are dark, and their legs are striped all the way down to their hooves.
(PLAINS ZEBRA)

CAPE MOUNTAIN ZEBRA
Equus zebra zebra

The Cape mountain zebra is the smallest zebra, standing only four feet at the shoulder. It has a strip of narrow stripes above the base of the tail, and a flap of skin on its neck called a *dewlap*.
(MOUNTAIN ZEBRA)

BURCHELL'S ZEBRA
Equus burchelli burchelli

HARTMANN'S MOUNTAIN ZEBRA
Equus zebra hartmannae

Hartmann's mountain zebras are taller than Cape mountain zebras, and their stripes are narrower and closer together.
(MOUNTAIN ZEBRA)

6

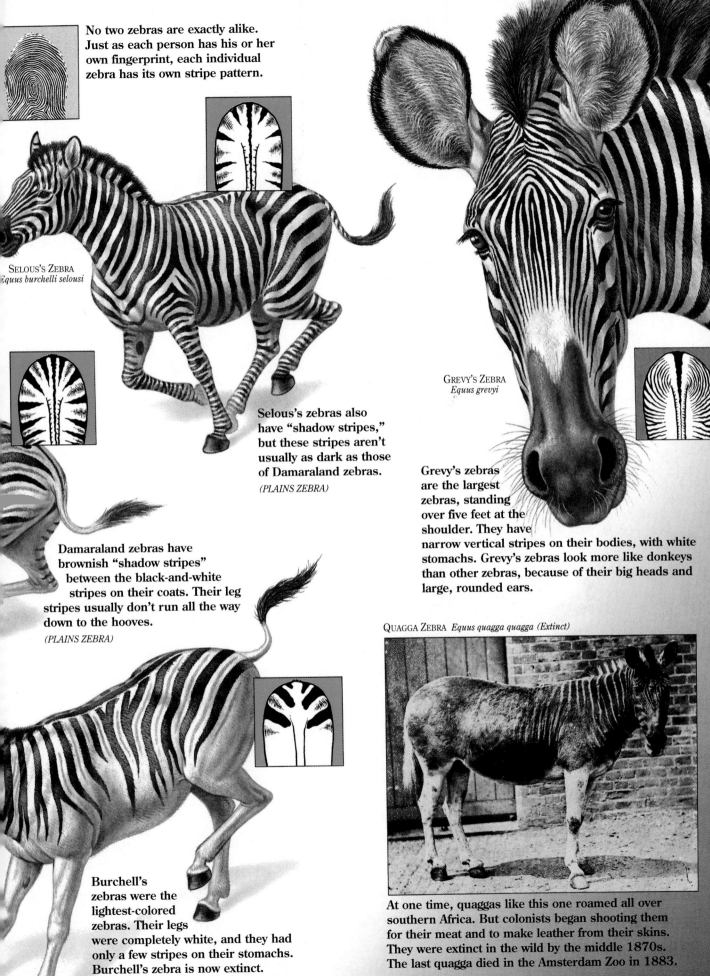

No two zebras are exactly alike. Just as each person has his or her own fingerprint, each individual zebra has its own stripe pattern.

SELOUS'S ZEBRA
Equus burchelli selousi

Selous's zebras also have "shadow stripes," but these stripes aren't usually as dark as those of Damaraland zebras.
(PLAINS ZEBRA)

Damaraland zebras have brownish "shadow stripes" between the black-and-white stripes on their coats. Their leg stripes usually don't run all the way down to the hooves.
(PLAINS ZEBRA)

GREVY'S ZEBRA
Equus grevyi

Grevy's zebras are the largest zebras, standing over five feet at the shoulder. They have narrow vertical stripes on their bodies, with white stomachs. Grevy's zebras look more like donkeys than other zebras, because of their big heads and large, rounded ears.

QUAGGA ZEBRA *Equus quagga quagga (Extinct)*

Burchell's zebras were the lightest-colored zebras. Their legs were completely white, and they had only a few stripes on their stomachs. Burchell's zebra is now extinct.
(PLAINS ZEBRA)

At one time, quaggas like this one roamed all over southern Africa. But colonists began shooting them for their meat and to make leather from their skins. They were extinct in the wild by the middle 1870s. The last quagga died in the Amsterdam Zoo in 1883.

A Grant's zebra grazes alongside her foal. They belong to one of four kinds of zebras that are called plains zebras because they live on the African plains.

Zebras are social animals. They live in small family groups of 5 to 15 animals. A family group is usually made up of several females and their young, led by an adult male, or *stallion*.

Living in groups is much safer for zebras than living alone. This is because several zebras have many more eyes and ears to watch and listen for predators. Also, if one zebra is in trouble, the others come to its rescue. And if a zebra is missing from the group, all search for it until it is found.

Sometimes fights break out between male zebras. Usually the animals try to bite each other on the neck and legs, or they kick each other with their hind legs. Fighting zebras can hurt each other seriously.

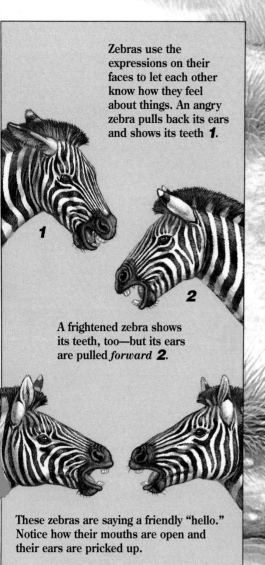

Zebras use the expressions on their faces to let each other know how they feel about things. An angry zebra pulls back its ears and shows its teeth **1**.

A frightened zebra shows its teeth, too—but its ears are pulled *forward* **2**.

These zebras are saying a friendly "hello." Notice how their mouths are open and their ears are pricked up.

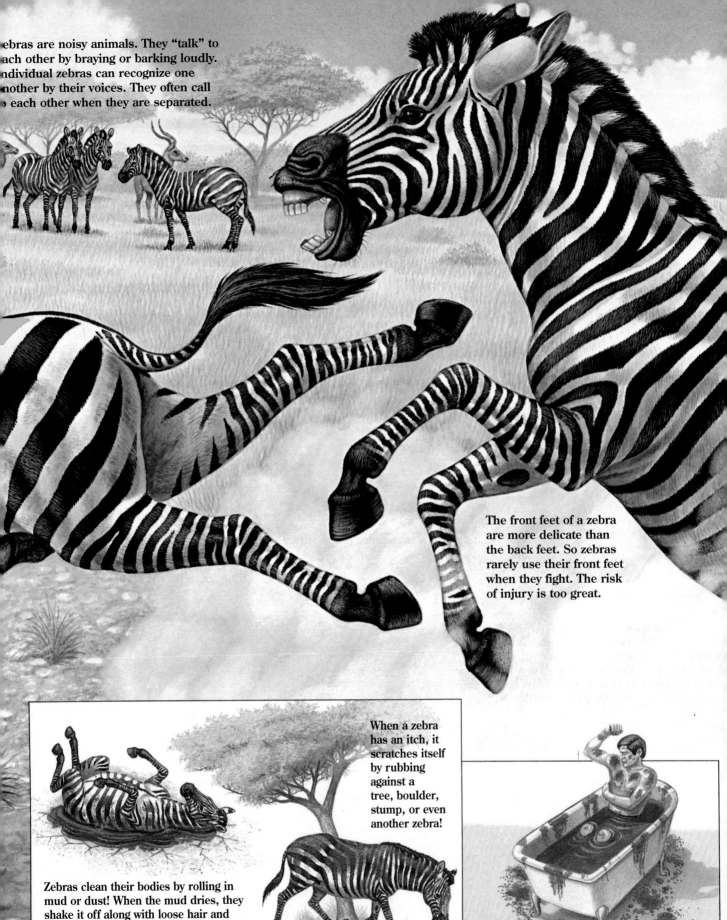

ebras are noisy animals. They "talk" to
ach other by braying or barking loudly.
ndividual zebras can recognize one
nother by their voices. They often call
 each other when they are separated.

The front feet of a zebra
are more delicate than
the back feet. So zebras
rarely use their front feet
when they fight. The risk
of injury is too great.

When a zebra
has an itch, it
scratches itself
by rubbing
against a
tree, boulder,
stump, or even
another zebra!

Zebras clean their bodies by rolling in
mud or dust! When the mud dries, they
shake it off along with loose hair and
flakes of dry skin. The film of dust that
is left on the skin acts as a shield
against heat, wind, and insects.

Wouldn't it be funny if you could clean yourself
the way zebras do—by taking a bath in mud?

Zebras are grazing animals. Their favorite food is grass. But if necessary, they will eat shrubs, leaves, fruit, roots, and even bark. Because this type of food is low in nutritional value, zebras must eat a lot of it to get the nourishment they need.

For this reason, they spend many hours each day grazing. But they always keep a watchful eye out for trouble. Usually they graze in the morning and late evening. Then at midday, they rest in the shade, standing together in a close group. When all the grass in one area has been eaten, they move on to new pastures.

Birds called oxpeckers help to keep zebras clean by eating the tiny pests that burrow in their skin.

Zebras need to drink water often. When water is scarce, they can sniff out underground pools, dig a hole, and uncover a fresh supply.

Zebras often graze side by side with wildebeests. Occasionally, they are seen with giraffes. When they eat, giraffes trim the treetops, and zebras and wildebeests clip the grass.

Some scientists think that a zebra's stripes help to hide, or *camouflage*, it within the herd. But predators seem to have no trouble picking out one zebra to chase. Do a zebra's stripes really make it harder for predators to see it? We may never know for sure.

When attacked by predators, an alarm call is passed through the herd and all the animals flee. As they run, they stay very close together, with their bodies almost touching. They can run this way for hours without ever bumping into one another.

Zebras almost never rest in tall grass, because a predator could be hiding there. When they do lie down to rest, one animal—usually a stallion—remains standing to watch for trouble.

Baby zebras are called *foals*. Male babies are called *colts*, and young females are called *fillies*. A newborn foal weighs 60 to 70 pounds and stands about 3 feet tall. Its fur is softer and fuzzier than its mother's is. And its stripes are sometimes brown and white, rather than black and white.

A mother zebra watches over her foal carefully and keeps it close to her at all times. When the foal is very young, she chases away any other zebra that comes near—even the leader of the group. When the foal grows older, it joins the rest of the small herd and plays with other young zebras. But even then, its mother and other adult zebras protect it from predators.

When danger threatens, the adults pus the foals to the inside of the herd to gu them. Then they all take off running, t babies safe within a mass of bodies.

Foals have manes that run down the whole length of their backs—all the way down to their tails. As a foal gets older, the long mane disappears, and an adult mane takes its place. But while the offspring is young, its mother grooms the mane often to show her affection.

Foals spend a lot of time playing. By running fast and pushing and shoving each other in play fights, they develop speed and strength. And they learn how to be leaders and followers and to run with the herd.

When running with the herd, foals always stay close to their mothers for protection. But other zebras watch over them, too—if necessary.

Within 15 minutes after it is born, a foal is up on its feet. Within an hour, it can run fast enough to keep up with the herd. It can do this because its legs are very long—almost as long as its mother's are. Baby zebras *must* be able to run soon after birth. Otherwise, they would be easy prey for predators.

A baby zebra has such long legs that it has to splay them like a giraffe when it wants a drink of water.

People are fascinated by the zebra's striped pattern. Ancient Romans kept zebras in their circuses and called them "horse-tigers" because of their stripes. And in 19th-century Europe, zebras sometimes pulled the carriages of royalty and other wealthy and fashionable people. The striped horses were popular in private zoos from England to India. The Empress Josephine kept a zebra in her private zoo, and her children regularly rode "zebraback."

Sadly, the two zebras that were the most popular in 19th-century Europe—the quagga and Burchell's zebra—were both extinct by the early 20th century. But the reason they became extinct was not because a few were taken into captivity. Hundreds of millions of herd animals—zebras and a variety of antelopes—once blanketed the southern plains of Africa. It seemed impossible that they would ever disappear. But within a few generations after colonists arrived, some species were extinct.

Until European exploration opened the African continent to the rest of the world, zebras and other animals lived in balance with one another and with the indigenous peoples of Africa. Zebras were killed by lions and hyenas and by people—but only for food and not in large enough numbers to harm the population.

Early in the 1800s, quaggas that had thundered across the Cape region of southern Africa in tens of thousands were being shot in such great numbers by Dutch colonists (known as Boers) that the balance of many animal populations was seriously disturbed. By mid-century, few quaggas were still alive. Farther to the north, Burchell's zebras were being killed in dramatic numbers. By the late 1870s, the quagga was extinct in the wild, and by 1920, Burchell's zebra was extinct.

These and other animals were exterminated by Boer farmers, who didn't want wild grazing animals to compete with their domestic sheep, goats, and cattle for food. The land had supported many wild grazing species because zebras eat the coarse tops of the grasses, wildebeest feast on the tender leaves and stems, and gazelles crop the lower shoots. Domestic grazers eat it all, slow new growth, and devastate the land.

Although Boer rifles methodically destroyed several animal species, there was one zebra—never numerous—that the Boers saved. In 1656, Jan van Riebeeck, the governor of the Cape of Good Hope, recognized that the Cape mountain zebra survived with only a small population and granted it protection. But when the British took over the Cape region in 1806, protection became lax, and the Cape mountain zebra seemed doomed to extinction.

Toward the end of the 1800s and the beginning of the 1900s, many people became concerned about disappearing wildlife, and international conservation groups were formed. Game management programs were later developed, and land set aside as national parks to protect wildlife and provide suitable habitats. Fortunately, the government of South Africa established Mountain Zebra National Park in 1937—the year that only 47 Cape mountain zebras remained. Six zebras were moved into the park, and private ranchers later helped boost the population with zebras they had protected on their own property.

Today, the Cape mountain zebra and Hartmann's mountain zebra are still endangered species, but through the efforts of governments, zoos, and private citizens, they do survive. And in Africa's many national parks, large herds of the plains zebras live alongside antelopes, buffaloes, elephants, and rhinos—as they once did throughout the grasslands of Africa. As we learn more about the earth and its inhabitants, it becomes clear that we also must learn to live in balance with nature.

ON THE COVER: Zebras

Series Created by
John Bonnett Wexo

Written by
Linda C. Wood

Scientific Consultant
Oliver Ryder, Ph.D.
Geneticist, Center for Reproduction
of Endangered Species (CRES)
Zoological Society of San Diego

CEO/Publisher
Penny Ertelt

Circulation Manager
Jay Hillis

Fulfillment Manager
Shirley Patiño

Customer Service
LaFonda Ryales
Irene Carroll
Carmel Valderrama

Controller
Cecil Kincaid, Jr.

Accountants
Sandra A. Battah
Paula Dennis

Online Marketing Manager
Debra S. Ives

Sales
Jenny Sparling
Dara Sivilay
Allan Gilbert
Robert Procell
Sally Mercer

Editorial Directors
Marjorie Shaw
Renee C. Burch

Production Artist
Jim Webb

Original Cover Design by
Mark Tolleshaug

Photographic Credits
Front Cover: Fulvio Eccardi (Bruce Coleman, Inc.); **Inside Front Cover and Page One:** Gerry Ellis (Globio); **Page Five: Top,** Brian Miller (Bruce Coleman, Inc.); **Right,** Frans Lanting (Minden Pictures); **Page Seven:** Zoological Society of London; **Pages Eight and Nine:** Stephen J. Krasemann (Photo Researchers); **Page Sixteen and Inside Back Cover:** Tim Davis (Photo Researchers).

Art Credits
All paintings by Richard Orr

AVAILABLE ZOOBOOKS TITLES:

Alligators & Crocodiles
Animal Babies
Animal Babies 2
Animal Champions
Animal Champions 2
Animal Wonders
Apes
Bats
Bears
Big Cats
Birds of Prey
Butterflies
Camels
Cheetahs
Chimpanzees
Deer Family
Dinosaurs
Dolphins & Porpoises
Ducks, Geese & Swans
Eagles
Elephants

Endangered Animals
Giant Pandas
Giraffes
Gorillas
Hippos
Hummingbirds
Insects
Insects 2
Kangaroos
Koalas & Other
Australian Animals
Lions
Little Cats
Nocturnal Animals
Old World Monkeys
Orangutans
Ostriches
Owls
Parrots
Penguins
Polar Bears

Rattlesnakes
Rhinos
Sea Otters
Seabirds
Seals & Sea Lions
Sharing the World
with Animals
Sharks
Skunks & Their
Relatives
Snakes
Spiders
Tigers
Turtles
Whales
Wild Dogs
Wild Horses
Wolves
Zebras

For more from Zoobooks please visit our website
www.Zoobooks.com

Published by Wildlife Education, Ltd.®

Wildlife Education, Ltd.
12233 Thatcher Court
Poway, California 92064-6880
www.zoobooks.com
800-477-5034

ISBN 0-937934-57-7

Printed in the U.S.A.